Exocarpalism

Jan Gutstein

METACARPALISM
Copyright © 2022 Dan Gutstein
All Rights Reserved.
Published by Unsolicited Press.
Printed in the United States of America.
First Edition.

No part of this book may be used or reproduced in any manner whatsoever without written permission except in the case of brief quotations embodied in critical articles or reviews. People, places, and notions in these stories are from the author's imagination; any resemblance is purely coincidental.

Attention schools and businesses: for discounted copies on large orders, please contact the publisher directly.

For information contact:
Unsolicited Press
Portland, Oregon
www.unsolicitedpress.com
orders@unsolicitedpress.com
619-354-8005

Cover Design: Kathryn Gerhardt
Editor: Alexandra Lindenmuth

ISBN: 978-1-956692-05-1

Thanks to the editors of these publications where the following poems first appeared (sometimes in slightly different form):

8 Poems: "The Emporium of Youth"
    and/or: "Interview at Wrong Number"
Beltway: A Poetry Quarterly: "On Sensitivity: A Brief
    Philosophy of Political Choice" and "Interview with
    Danish Kroner"
Café Irreal: "Fourteen Periods (for Clarice Lispector)"
DIAGRAM: "(C)harm City"
Gargoyle: "The Windowpanes of Phantom Addresses" and
"Ineffable"
Mad Hatter's Review Mad Hat Lit: "Interview with a Nudist
    Who Has Never Been Undressed by Anyone's Eyes"
PANK: "Das Lunchmeats"; "Dearth, Incorporated"; "Sugar in
    the Raw": "Demographics"; "Labour Saving Devices";
    "Beef Pineapple Robot"; and "To Kick a Mockingbird's
    Ass"
The Prose Poem Project: "Takeout Bakeout"
Upstairs at Duroc: "Metacarpalism"
Voicemail Poems: "Interview with a Yes Man"

Several of these poems appeared in a chapbook, *Alt Tk*, published by Dusie Kollektiv.

To my friend Lieutenant Mike "The Torpedo" Zito, aka "Sausages"

For his tireless reading of these poems and for being a righteous human being.

Contents

Interview with Danish Kroner	1
By Saying "I'm Sleeping with Someone,"	2
Live Blogging from Negotiations between the Rapper, Ice-T, and the Restaurant Chain, T.G.I. Fridays, over the Menu for Their Joint Venture, Ice-T.G.I. Fridays	3
I've Got That on My Radar	5
Top 7 Reactions When Counting to 60 by Units of 1-Mississippi	7
When a Flora Eats a Fauna	9
Da Botch	11
Dearth, Incorporated	12
(C)harm City	13
Rowboats in the Woods	14
Interview with the Official in Charge of Estimating Delay	15
Metacarpalism	16
Yes, Maybe You're Not a Leftist	17
Notes (for Sonnet)	19
Best Practices During My Recent Interaction with a Bat	22
The Windowpanes of Phantom Addresses	24
Interview at Wrong Number	26
8 Tips on How to Write a Great Story (+1 "Obvi")	

(+1 Solution)	27
Communication Breakdown: An Eco-Friendly Parable	29
Parts Per Million: An Open Letter to Climate Change Skeptics Who Do Not, in Turn, Reject the Science of Warfare	32
The Emporium of Youth	34
Interview with a Nudist Who Has Never Been Undressed by Anyone's Eyes	35
L=A=N=G=U=I=S=H Poetry	36
Das Lunchmeats	38
Beef Pineapple Robot	40
Demographics	41
To Kick a Mockingbird's Ass	42
Labour Saving Devices	43
Études, Brute?	44
Pollstergeist	46
Interview with a Yes Man	48
For Dissidence	50
Essay after Another Episode of Angry Prejudice	53
Prayer for a Former Student Who Clings to Life in an Unknown Hospital	55
Teaching the Cannon	57
The Doctrine Is IN.	59
Takeout Bakeout	60
Consider Tense When Observing a Horse	61

List of Rejected Conspiracy Theories	62
Interview with a Volunteer Who Just Wants to Give Back to the Community	63
Preponderances	64
Fourteen Periods (for Clarice Lispector)	65
What's Comin' Atcha	66
Under Armoire	68
Rimbaud: First Blood	69
Postmodern Tentacle Liturgy	70
Sugar in the Raw	71
OfayCupid	72
Interview with a Child in Time Out	73
On Sensitivity: A Brief History of Political Choice	74
Oh, There Are Hearts	75
Everything's a Burger	77
Blue Jay-Z	78
Ineffable	79
Moments De-installed from Servitude	81
People Who Don't Listen to Music	82
What I Lost Was This:	84
Why I Love Poets	85

Interview with Danish Kroner

I am looking for the warm wine
I was told "Come, come! we'll serve warm wine
& there will be many kippered fish, too"
please point me toward the kippered fish
I confess ignorance of this tradition where
a common egg is apparently pickled
(purple) & kept in a large jar w/ many purple eggs
does each partygoer receive a pickled food item
before the sing-along? b/c
there might be quite a delay as guests are
seated at the table according to name cards
invariably a partygoer will remark &
I will respond: Yes, that is my Christian Name &
no, I am not aware of the prevailing exchange rate.

By Saying "I'm Sleeping with Someone,"

the fellow means he's sleeping with the fragrance of her hair at repose, the forward jut of her hip bones, the restlessness of her feet kicking the tympanic surface of the mattress. He's sleeping with the contours of her embryonic familiarity.

The thundering noise from above is, in fact, thunder, if we define thunder with the generous elasticity that thunder generates, sequentially. A hawk lingers on an arterial wire. It was built in a rainstorm, the hawk's plumage is rainfall, its mid-air colors and runoff.

A glancing moment, as when a boxer must claw the struggle for viability within the emergency of his own footing. His opposite smites the blundering footage underneath his wobbly mentality, an idea that implies the spark of a knuckle upon the recalcitrant chin.

Your child years, your work years, your aged years. What a catastrophe—to need—to take action, the way bells and horns regulate the sluggish ambulation of conveyances bound for a hub, a destination-hub, the afternoon never able to clear or clarify its ambiguities.

Live Blogging from Negotiations between the Rapper, Ice-T, and the Restaurant Chain, T.G.I. Fridays, over the Menu for Their Joint Venture, Ice-T.G.I. Fridays

It's all Ice-T. He rejects *fa*jitas in favor of *pho*jitas. The corporate attorneys tap their tablets. "I want *Nice*-Tea, on he *drinks* menu," he says, "in *France*." When the attorneys don't get it, their faces begging for the brutality of an explanation, he emphasizes "*Niece*-Tea. In *France*." He makes two-handed typing motions to the attorneys, who oblige. Someone chants, "Clobber you with a sizzlin' skillet / *pho*jita in a fizzlin' minute," but the room's so packed, it's not clear who rapped. The space glows with blue cigarette vapor and stuffed polished ashtrays and shiny sharkskin zoot suits. Ice-T questions the "G" in T.G.I. Fridays. He thinks it should be "O.G." as in "Thank Original Gangster It's Fridays." He asks them to double-check the grammar—"Y'all went to *Yale* or whatever"—while the attorneys type. It's all Ice-T. "But if we do keep *God*," he emphasizes, "gotta be deity *neutral* gotta be *mono*-deity neutral." He adds, "*Dieu* as you please, civil *play*," while one of his homies slaps him a low five. The room quiets but for the ever-present tapping of tablets. "Y'all better not be doing *Facebook*," cautions the rapper. They get back to the menu. "I want Ice-T-Bone steak," says the rapper. "I want Ice-TV Dinner and Ice-TIAA-Cref for all the employees and Ice-TT Shaker on the speakers overhead: there, and there." He spreads out his arms in benediction. It's all Ice-T. He's regulating. The attorneys haven't been so humbled. They all wear the same laissez faire eyeglasses and the same Titanic haircuts and the same chokers around their necks. Someone raps, "Gonna diss your stereo / It's gonna be Blau*punkt*," but it's not clear who's speaking, with so many entourages huddling at every distance. Ice-T turns to his counsel. "Yo, I want outta Law & Order," he goes. "See about that Miami Vice-T idea." Suddenly, the rapper Pitbull appears, on the right hand of the Fridays CEO. "*Oh hell no*," says Ice-T, who stands. Everyone stands, except the attorneys, whose offshore helter shelter faces once again require the brutality of an explanation. "Now, Tracy," says the Fridays CEO, but Ice-T bristles at the mention of his given name. "Who we got here?" he says. "*Pitfall*? Red Bull? Bull *bleep* winkle?" It's like the weigh-in of a prizefight, with Ice-T and Pitbull standing so close, each man can see his face in the other man's irises. "No Dice-T," says Pitbull. "It's *fa*jita, not *pho*jita." Ice-T thinks this over, not blinking. "One condition," he goes. "*Theme* park. Out back. Ice-Tee time for my golfers. Ice-Tee ball for the little ones. Ice-Tee shirt concession." Pitbull winces. The attorneys offer cigars to their colleagues. Everyone claps. It's all Ice-T. He's regulating. Out comes Ice-Téa Leoni, dressed in a very revealing waitress kit, offering a slushy for everyone. The cameras flash in Ice-T's face. He could have anything. His own political party. The Ice-Tea Party. But he's affable, as is. Yes, affable will do. Yes, it will. It will suffice-T.

I've Got That on My Radar

—I've got that on my radar.
—Me, too.
—Do other people have it on their radars?
—Everyone has this on his or her radar.

—Remember the days of *no* radar?
—What was there if there was *no* radar?
—Carburetors?
—Faithfulness?

—Heh heh heh.
—Heh heh heh.
—When my girlfriend moved in, she kept her radar.
—More women are keeping their radars these days.

—Do you see blips?
—Only when I stand up too quickly.
—Sometimes when I'm alone, I hear applause.
—Maybe you've got The Clap.

—Okay, I've got that on my radar.
—Do you have it on your sonar?
—Should I have it on my sonar?
—The sea ice, after all, is melting. . .

—Do you have that on your deep space probe?
—I'm not sure I care for that phrase.
—(...)
—(...)

—Does *man* drum in the woods?
—Do *you* drum in the woods?
—I have no drum. There are no woods.
—Then you must throw percussion to the wind!

Top 7 Reactions When Counting to 60 by Units of 1-Mississippi

[1.] Why Mississippi?

You got your 1-Arid Desert, 2-Arkansas, 3-Micronesia, 4-Tea Party, 5-Global Warming, 6-Federal Debt, 7-Mississippi, 8-Lewis & Clark's Route to the Pacific, 9-Colorado River Basin in Crisis, 10-Took a Wooden Nickel, you know? There's a lot of ways to count to 60. So OK so.

[2.] Shouldn't you begin with "Zero-Mississippi"?

It's not like the Universe began, and it was already 1-Mississippi outside. No, it was less than 1. Headed there, but not yet 1. So, I mean, shouldn't you go "Zero Mississippi"? What would the world be like without Mississippi? Delta-less? Delta blues-less? See? It's more than you think.

[3.] There's an infinite amount of time between 0 and 60.

Don't believe me? Divide a half in half. You get half & half. They call it half & half because it comes out of a cow that has mixed ethnicity. Whole milk, on the other hand, comes out of a pure-bred cow. They have both types in Mississippi, pure cows and halfies. Lots o' cows, yep.

[4.] Does anybody ever make it to 60, and if so, who?

I bet that Gandhi counted to 60 a few times, although I doubt that he ever said "Mississippi." They have a statue of him in Washington, D.C. In the statue, he braces himself with a walking stick and wears a thin wrap. I worry about him when it gets below freezing. He must be mighty cold!

[5.] The 1960s is a distant target.

You could count to the 1960s by year and by Mississippi, so you could go "1900-Mississippi, 1901-Mississippi," and so forth, but by "1960-Mississippi" you'd be too exhausted to enjoy John Coltrane's music, which transformed so much turmoil into beauty ... but I digress.

[6.] What does each unit of 1-Mississippi indicate?

The lightning is 3-Mississippi away. You are 1 Mississippi closer to chasing your friends. In 9-Mississippi the CEO will issue a public statement but will shy away from making an apology. It takes Umpteen-Mississippi to achieve happiness unless you experience Premature-Mississippi.

[7.] Let's try the Stuff Smith Counting Game in French.

One = un. Two = deux. Three = trois, et cetera. So OK so: Un-deux// trois-quatre// cinq-six// uh-huit// neuf-woof. Which is how a lot of French ends, with silliness like neuf-woof. You don't get silliness when counting via 1-Mississippi. You just never get to 60. But at least you have your dignity!

When a Flora Eats a Fauna

A flora develops carnivorous knowledge, and it spreads, this knowledge, in hedgerows and alpine forests and scrub formations throughout the land, a fauna disappearing here and there—a real head-scratcher to the schools, bales, coveys, clutches, packs, prides, tribes, colonies, sleuths, and bloats, until one flora, one day, entraps a fauna in public, on the side of the road: the fauna, sitting there, in the flora's gullet, thinking, "Aw, man, what'll happen to my radical politics *now*?" Other fauna stand at a distance from the victim, who nods at them in the country manner. "Well, this explains everything," says one in the crowd. "Not everything," says another. "It doesn't explain Wal-Mart, Wall Street, and Kmart, and it hardly explains the general misallocation of resources." Another in the crowd addresses the victim: "What's it like in there?" The victim replies, "Itchy." A second questioner says, "Itchy or ticklish?" The victim says, "It's making me sneeze. I think I'm allergic to being digested." The sun sets and the sun rises. Some of the fauna drift off to eat a flora, in the hopes that the predatory flora would change its mind and release their kin-fauna, while others drift off to eat other fauna. The sun sets and the sun rises. Now but a few fauna maintain a vigil at the site of the entrapment. They kindle candles, they chant verses, they clutch teddy bears. "How's it going?" one of the vigilant asks the victim. "Not bad," says the victim. "Basically, I'm content. I feel like I can be digested and move on with my life." Another of the vigilant asks, "Are you stuck? You look a little stuck." The victim thinks this over. "I am experiencing very, very slow peristalsis, whatever that means. So, yeah. I think I'm stuck." The sun sets and the sun rises. None of the fauna remain at the site of the entrapment, leaving behind all the materials of their vigil: hollowed out candles; heaps of department store bears; and a jumble of Starbucks take-out cups, raw sugar packets, and wooden stirs. "I guess this is it," the victim thinks. "Not all herbs are herbivores. It gets so—you want to tax everything and hide in the cellar. It's a cellar's market, after all." He thinks no more. He becomes, for a moment, the flora's ornament: apple-headed, stubborn, and frozen in mild recognition of some great folly, before the flora, sort of, introduces the fauna into the very fiber of its fiber, acquiring in the digested fauna the essential fears and contradictions of its faunal kingdom, while around the flora wheels a watery wind that will nourish the vegetation in its growing polemic—a brash, wasteful imperialism that startles the very purity of the floral roots.

Da Botch

The bus driver, once again, flips the pedestrian "the bird." So, the pedestrian *rides* the bus, figuring: "He can't give me the bird anymore because I'm *riding* the bus." Then, the bus driver slams on the brakes, and the pedestrian— "Oooh!" she says—falls out the door. She's a pedestrian again, and the bus driver is always the bus driver, he's always been the bus driver. He gives her the bird. She takes the new route home, but there's always a bus, and in that bus, under the little lamp, there's usually a bus driver, who flips her the bird. "Is it in their job descriptions," she thinks, "to flip me the bird?" She buys a can of black spray-paint but doesn't really know what she's doing. She shakes it, rattling those little balls in the can, and sprays a terrible doodle on the wall, the wall of the newspaper building, the newspaper that always tells you what you think they're gonna tell you. She yells at her boyfriend that night, and he says, "yeah yeah yeah." The next day, she yells at a colleague, too, over an ambiguous break room encounter. The colleague has a tattoo, just above the sock-line, that reads, "Beers beers beers." She thinks "yeah yeah yeah," she thinks "beers beers beers." She would invoke the loud legend of her God, but he's at the track, playing the ponies, or he's at the track, wearing a fedora, with his stinky armpit stains. She steps into the evening, just as the bus drifts down the street. "NOT IN SERVICE," it goes, on its forehead, passing her without incident, but leaving her, clap, clop, to walk the city in Autumn chill.

Dearth, Incorporated

Behold the Drought. It loiters and we forget.
We engage in abominations while the Drought endures.
The rains must come if the rains don't come.
If the rains don't come the rains must come.
You know the rest. The cucumbers parch beside the heirlooms.
The vegetarian goes without.
He must sample a little turkey, instead.
He must chew a little tender, juicy bird. Behold the Drought.
The lip of it to the north of Danville, Va.,
amongst all the Danville Gals.
A beachhead to the west of Ocean City, N.J.,
amongst all the Danville Gals.
It loiters, the Drought, and we forget. We water our crabgrass.
Nudge our grabass. Bed down beside our false idols.
The Neo-Stoics postulate that water, itself, thirsts,
and assert the stratagem.
The rains must come if the rains don't come.
If the rains don't come the rains must come.
Shortages is Shortages. That's the plan.
"For sayings ye are, and unto sayings shall ye return."
We engage in abominations while the Drought endures:
Senator, Senator, Senator, Senator, Senator.

(C)harm City

An arm thrown around defunct machinery.
The prevalence of sorrow,
sorrow as common ambience.
What stoppages a grid offers,
what off-ramps.
The pale, sifted orange of afternoon windows.
The pale, sifted orange of careful thinking.
The same clouds for two weeks.
It needs to rain, and it rains,
dotty fabric, the rain.
Not enough to discredit the integrity of structures, okay.
Okay, a vehicle cannot pass-through another vehicle.
A towering support isn't two, but one.
The skin of obedience as opposed to the metastasis of anger.
How many ways to beg, "No."
An insinuation of relief
despite the full moon of a lamppost
be-glittering the sidewalk purified by a victim,
just leaking blood.
And the footsteps, the babble of footsteps
in too many directions, to be understood. . .

Rowboats in the Woods

Are you in-country or incontinent?
Is your auntie's bedroom an auntie chamber?
Do you fuck the fascists?
What is the rate of error with man-made lakes?
How can I overcome institutional inertia?
Who were the forebears of The Three Bears?
Isn't the bullet harvested the way the potato is harvested?
To the wounded, who insists upon stitching his own wound:
    'ok, suture self!'

Why are there rowboats in the woods?
Is it a moon-colored day or a rain-colored day?
Can a bird be both scarf and insinuation?
Why does a person mourn within the apparatus of erosion?
What will our brothers be singing?
What will our brothers be singing,
    as we return their bodies to the earth?

Interview with the Official in Charge of Estimating Delay

Yep, we outsourced Estimation in the 90s & the Aughts to Samoa, or so we thought, but when the phone records came back Albania, well, that scandal kicked the calories outta Middle Management & we brought that job home I mean, one job, I know it ain't much, but I'm proud to say by now, these Delays are 100 percent American Made & 100 percent American Estimated & 100 percent American Middle Managed & 100 percent American Fulfilled—that is, when the Delayed equipment, person, or sum actually arrives (I was sent to Theory Courses at the Extension Campus & ever since I've adopted the motto: Keeping It Real Time!) Oh yes ma'am you can expect a delay of 10 to 15 minutes our latest information suggests a delay of 20 to 25 minutes, see? I just love helping a Fellow Citizen to be Delayed.

Metacarpalism

Differentiate between "I thought it" and "I said it to myself."
Did you think "torrid" or did you say "torrid" to yourself?
The value of "torrid" is irrelevant
except to note that Žižek cannot aid you any longer,
if he aided you ever, at all.
Clays, as verb, would be more assistive: he clays,
she clays (together) the theory of devotion, for example,
amidst the various "systems of devotion."
Theories, that is, versus actual deference,
which brings me to Metacarpalism.
There are five metacarpals in each hand,
offering us ten ways to translate our persistent concavity—
if only you'll shiver off the euphoria.
Please, please, please shiver off the euphoria, now.
If you were post-structural ever, at all,
you might consider puncturing the glass and plunging
the big red button that proclaims: Deconstruct.
Derrida cannot aid you any longer.
Did you think "differentiate"
or did you say "differentiate" to yourself?
One curvilinear form maps itself to another curvilinear form.
That's called correlation; it's renewable.
Facts about the metacarpals will not open your hand.
Metacarpal Diem: Open your hand.

Yes, Maybe You're Not a Leftist

Are you left-brine or right-brine dominant?
It would depend upon which ocean you await.
The Atlantic always approaches shore from right to left whereas
the Pacific always approaches shore from left to right.
Oceans force you to adopt the same stance,
no matter how you might strive to politicize an issue.
Our centrists must reside in the middle of the continent—
they count both the artist and the analyst among their ranks.
An apple can the centrists paint.
A standard deviation can the centrists compute.
Would you apply Right Guard to your right-side armpit,
or in general, to conservative body odor?
Oh, would there be Left Guard for the left-side armpit
or for the perspiration of liberals, who continue to perspire,
apparently, without remediation. Personally,
I blame this problem on our two-armpit system.
Not that a third armpit could stagger the political impasse,
except maybe in a matted hair environment,
where an alternative might break the dreadlocks.
Do you think that the famous French bell-ringer
drives the Hatchback of Notre Dame?
Maybe he prefers to ride the Quasi-Moto-Cycle.
In France, the Atlantic approaches shore from left to right,

forcing citizens to be right-brine dominant,
les droitiers. There, the donkey brays,
the chefs braise, the Frenchies tilt their berets.

Notes (for Sonnet)

(1)

Greeks do not like Al Gore, former V.P., U.S.A. Al Gore at the Autobus Stop, Al Gore at the Tzatziki Vendor, Al Gore in Athens. No! This could result in Al-Gore-A-Phobia.

(2)

Received a citation for "Disturbing the Cod-Peace," by Officer (Miss) Demeanor. Told to leave that cod-peace in extra virgin turmoil. Or was it extroversion term oil?

(3)

Decide between (a) Rockin' the Casbah & (b) Rockin' the Cash Bar. Regarding Schlitz Malt Liquor Istanbul. Dwayne Johnson?—The Rock?—in the Casbah? (Skip.)

(4)

Jumping ship became an art form. Sailors as artists tossing themselves into the cold, cold briny. Shipmates to holler "Man Oeuvre Board!" when considering entire bodies of work.

(5)

The Hind-Lick Maneuver, The Heinz-Lick Maneuver, Orchestral Manures in the Dark, Heimlich Manure, Military Manures, The Hymie Lick Maneuver.

(6)

So, a guy named Walter bought a gate. Note: that would be Walter's Gate. It didn't keep out Republicans. Then came Congressional "Probe." Then came "Special" Prosecutor.

(7)

Von Bismarck has been kidnapped! It's grand theft Otto!

(8)

If the Autobahn is where Germans can *drive* as fast as they please, then is The Audubon where birds can *fly* as fast as they please?

(9)

"Hey Bro. Did the other Bros steal all the pasta from the sorority house?" "Yeah Bro." "So, they carried out the Penne Raid?" "It was such a Penne Raid!" "Cool Bro." "You know it Bro." (Skip.)

(10)

NASA hiring astronaughts & expecting missions to succeed! Why not rocket the hip-hop musician, Nas, into space? Shorten NASA to NAS. Best idea since Big Ben Gay Talese.

(11)

SUNY-Previn *sucks*, the cafeteria smells like *wet dogs*, the dorms are *gross* & the quad is full of *douchebags*. Should I transfer to Rutgers-Hauer? RISD-Snider?

(12)

Retreats used to be full-scale military disgraces. Now you don't even leave the office and you order-in Buca di Beppo. The dog expects a second treat nowadays; a re-treat.

(13)

Who log-ins? Kenny? Kenny log-ins? How many Kenny log-ins? What? Log-ins & Messina? How many Log-ins & Messina? Huh? The Messina comin'? Land O' Lakes & Honey!

(14)

I need a prescription filled immediately. I need Apothecary Now. Then I called A.A. for a tow. "Al-Gore-A-Phobia Anonymous," said a man named Stavros. Honest mistake!

Best Practices During My Recent Interaction with a Bat

(1.)

A few nights ago, a bat fell out of the ice rain onto my jogging hoodie. It scrambled under my left armpit and began to groom itself there, upside down. I say "groom itself" but I have no idea what kind of batty things were going on, except for this moonstruck energy in a ticklish region. I jogged along, giggly, a bat clinging to my armpit, in the ice rain.

(2.)

There were, like, twenty stoic deer between me and the woods along Mass Ave., some with antlers. The deer looked at me like it was crazy to be anything but a deer in the ice rain, or any other night-weather. So, I slugged the bat with a fast hook to its little upside-down head. It didn't fly away. It dropped behind me. I heard it plop into an icy puddle.

(3.)

I thought the bat might flap me down, so I ran hard, but no fangs nipped my neck, trying to Dracularize me. I jogged past the newly erected statue of Nelson Mandela, his fist raised, bouquets at his feet. It seemed disrespectful to have clubbed a mammal near the memorial for such a peaceful man, but that's life—if you've got a bat on your hoodie!

(4.)

The next day, I went to the market, so I might select a roasting fowl. I got distracted by all the roaming these fowls had done. Several fowls had free-roamed the barn. Other fowls had free-roamed the range. They were expensive, on account of roaming fees. Yet not free enough: one of them birds went into my stew pot.

(5.)

Yes, I stewed a roasting fowl (FML but it was good!). I spent the rest of the day improving my skill sets: my Reaction to Annoyance, Analysis of Crucial Sporting Play, and Drinking Buddy Skills. In particular, my Drinking Buddy Skill Set has come a long way. Tell salty joke, pretend to hear above din, tap shot on bar before shooting. Yep.

(6)

I would like to issue a statement about the bat: It probably fluttered into a tree. I doubt its night was terribly unusual. While bats probably don't spend much time in armpits, they do spend half their lives stunned by human reactions. Would I do anything differently next time? Yeah, I'd throw that bat on those deer. They were far too stoic for it to be a human paradise.

The Windowpanes of Phantom Addresses

Homely streets terminate
at the windowpanes of phantom addresses.
A bit of salt in the clouds.

What percentage the blood from metals?
A scream, a siren, the two together before the scream alone.

Purpose crossing purpose
as when the purpose of haste crosses
the purpose of defenselessness
in the witch light of early condemnations.

(The confetti of isolation.)

The single color where upper and lower distance
cannot continue as distance.
There were three stars in the evening sky.
"Let us kiss three times—and all will be forgiven."

Proximity might be painful,
but echolocation requires a neighborhood,
an everyday bird climbing through mistranslation.

A stripe of sky campaigns between a block of cold rooftops
and the westerly hull of a warm cloud.

(Interior man, limited man, static.)

A helicopter rattles in the rustiness of its own levity,
bucking above a plain grid.

The taxicab driver remembered a boxer, Ike,
he could dance, and he could sting,
the meter nickeling a fare.

Interview at Wrong Number

Who is that? Danger?
Huh? Is that Danger?
I know it's you. Say
something! Chester?
Is that you? Is that
Chester? Who is that?
It's either Danger or
it's Chester, unless it's
Uncle Perp. Speak up!
Is that Uncle Perp?
Huh? Whoever it is
better give back my
damn ankle bracelet,
man, the cops're here!

8 Tips on How to Write a Great Story (+1 "Obvi") (+1 Solution)

(1) Don't describe sex blow by blow. At the very most, close the door and talk about the thumping against the headboard, but don't even do that. I once heard a novelist (who had a lisp) read a scene: "He gasthp't, she gasthp't!" Enough said.

(2) Don't say Budweiser ever in a story, especially if the "hero" is drinking it. For that matter, don't say tall boys, long necks, dead soldiers, Coors, Miller, or Tuborg Gold.

(3) If you have to have a weeping character, don't say "the tears rolled down his cheek." For god's sakes, man, quantum physics dictates that, in one out of every 100 crying jags, the tears will roll *up* the cheek.

(4) There's something in mainstream American fiction about "quiet" stories with vases of flowers on a dinner table. Really? I hereby outlaw flowers, vases, and tables.

(5) Avoid overuse of the verb "to be." Was this, were that, be this, is that, been who, are what? The sentences were, was, was, was, were.

(6) If you're going to write-in Irish characters, please don't have them say "fook" or "feck" half the time. I doubt Irish people say "fook" or "feck" half the time, but even if they do, it doesn't automatically make for good fiction.

(7) If something bad happens, say, an assassin hopping out of the curtains, don't instruct a character to say "Nooooo!" in response. Any of the following—"Huh" or "You don't say" or "I've waited for this all my life"—would be more surprising.

(8) I'm all for odd character names, but let's not get too crazy, okay? A woman named Bubonia or Boeing may be accurate on some level, but will the reader be able to maintain appropriate decorum in the face of such a *nom de guerre*?

(9) If you don't have a first sentence that establishes a situation, conflict, or problem, then you don't have a good first sentence. "Obvi!"

(10) Okay, so if your story describes two characters having sex in a room filled with Budweiser empties while one character is crying with his tears going up his cheek while a vase of flowers marinates on a table-top—was a vase? were it a vase?—and the other character said "fook me!" just before an assassin named Boeing jumps out of the curtains, forcing the other character to say "Nooooo!" all of this in the very first sentence, then yes, okay, that might make for a good story. Congrats.

Communication Breakdown: An Eco-Friendly Parable

After the Despot ordered the defenestration of his political rival, he retired to his bedchambers clad in deniability sleepwear—earplugs and blindfold—as he planned to claim "I heard nothing, I saw nothing" should the meek judiciary ever issue subpoenas. A noisy night of sawing, chopping, and chipping ensued, but the Despot slept like a sack of spuds. When the leader awoke, he wished to experience the symphonic triumph of the mid-morning sunlight. He threw the curtains apart, but imagine his Munch-scream face when he discovered that the woods—the *entire* woods—had vanished, a column of trucks grunting forward in low gear, each vehicle bearing a pyramid of thick trunks. On television, the Despot's political rival cemented the disgrace, the deforestation, by branding the Despot an enemy of the root, branch, wood, creature, creation, universe, God.

[2]
"Despot here," the leader hollered into the red telephone. "What the hell has happened?" Happened, sir? said his deputy. "What the hell have you done?" As you decreed, sir. The Despot's face softened, as if an unpleasant odor had been released. "What have I decreed?" he asked. The act has been carried out. And with considerable efficiency, I might add. "I ordered a defenestration." Yes, sir. "You have effected a deforestation, instead." Sir? "The forest," said the Despot, "is *missing*." Yes, sir. We defenestrated the forest, as you decreed. Sir, added the deputy, your political rival telephoned us this morning. He has challenged you to epee.

"Epee?" Yes, sir. "You mean, sword?" It's a foil, sir, it's an epee. "Impossible. I have no foil!" Well, sir, we could purchase one using EpeePal.

[3]

The Despot received embassies from noon until 1:00, after which he received audiences from 1:00 until 2:00, whereupon he received embassies from 2:00 until 3:00, inasmuch as he received lobbies. Representatives from the prophylactics industry spoke to the Despot about cornering the market for equine rubbers to prevent the conception of unwanted foals. They would produce, on a trial-basis, a condom billed as Trojan Horse. A group representing the nation's trawlers encouraged the Despot to seize the fish: *carp diem*, they implored. The leader bade his fool approach. Yo, I'm so impoverished, quipped the fool, I ain't got no despot to piss in. Trumpets signaled the embassies, audiences, and lobbies to toss many banknotes into a circulating hat. The Despot had listened to these visitors; they must subsidize his scrutiny; they must "pay attention."

[4]

That evening, the Despot sat with his soothsayer in the conservatory. "It's quite simple," said the Despot. "They heave my adversary out the window." Yes, sir, agreed the soothsayer. "They don't demolish an entire wooded region." Yes, sir, agreed the soothsayer. "Defenestration. Deforestation. Not the same!" The soothsayer hovered his palms over the leader's head, as if it were a crystal ball. I see your political rival practicing epee with corked tip, he hummed. "You do?" Yes, sir, the soothsayer hummed: quirky his thrust shall be. Just then, the fool appeared over the Despot's opposite shoulder. "How now?" said the Despot. He who places confidence in the soothsayer's racket, said the fool, shall become, himself, a *seer-sucker*. Dig? Nesting birds brawled in livid riffs on the slopes of roof. There were, after all, no more treetops.

Parts Per Million: An Open Letter to Climate Change Skeptics Who Do Not, in Turn, Reject the Science of Warfare

For the sake of Brevity, let us define Science as both Military and Climate. A belief in the routines of synthesizing Modern Weaponry, for example, would obligate you to believe in Global Warming. You couldn't believe in one part of Science, that is, without believing in all parts of Science, and in any event, for the sake of Brevity, we are offering a definition that equates, say, the Fundamental Routines required to conceive of Ordnance and Trajectory with the Fundamental Routines required to measure the levels of Greenhouse Gasses. Interestingly enough, the increased administration of Modern Weaponry will probably lead to the progression of Global Warming, and the progression of Global Warming will probably lead to the increased administration of Modern Weaponry. The scene shifts to a mountaintop in Hawai'i, where the measurement of Carbon in Parts Per Million surpasses reasonable levels. The polluted air—steeply—warms the earth yet you deny the Science. "This is natural," you may assert or "Mono-Deity intends for this to happen" or "Scientists Are Engaging in a Conspiracy to Falsify Their Findings" even as drastic consequences loom and the fossilized, ice-core history of the Earth hasn't indicated such disastrous levels of Parts Per Million in Millions of Years. Science, of course, builds cartridges, magazines, firearms, torque, detonations, submarines, jump jets, nerve agents, mushroom clouds, satellite guidance, and all sorts of sundry materiel. This is "Natural?" This is Mono-Deity? In one half of our basic two-part system, Science warns of Great Harm, and in the other half, Science produces Great Harm. You reject the former but not the latter. It must be nice to entitle yourselves to these types of inconsistencies. The scene shifts to man-made structures—rails, overpasses, domiciles, high-rises, signals, gutters, power plants, wiring, cathedrals, off ramps—that are, desperately, perpetually, attempting to crumble or combust. The scene shifts to soil, there is a Drought in the soil, the Drought rises toward the surface through soil that is perpetually striving to evaporate, and without some Immediate Attention, Skeptics, witness the Dumb Animal in Collapse.

The Emporium of Youth

Seen from another angle as when an area—
station, square—contemplated on a Sunday.
The expression may calcify into a demonstration
of thistle-thorn dismay. By "imagine your face"
I mean "shadow," your expression itself a shadow.
These colors: sky, stone, graffiti: these colors now.
The emporium of youth versus the emporium
of adulthood. If Person A will ail at Point X,
then Person B will ail at Point Y. (Loneliness
aggrandizes the symmetrical nature of most pain.)
Whereas a big galosh of dirty cloud busts open
a caucus of old doves. Brighten the ticking synapses
versus what warms the solid-state capacity for violence.
These colors: stone, wood, tower: these colors now.
The difference between idling (unit of riverbank)
and waiting (unit of high-rise). Rust, rusty coloring,
what gnaws into our porticos of awareness.
By "imagine your face," I mean the uncorrected
ritual of love. Or the sliding scale of sunlight,
or the balloting of voices in airshafts and alleys.

Interview with a Nudist Who Has Never Been Undressed by Anyone's Eyes

I waited for the bus so long my transfer expired.
When the bus finally arrived a radicalized youth
chucked a rock at it (clank!) & it swerved into traffic.
"Young Man!" I shouted, but he glared at me in a way
that knocked my body out of my body & I witnessed
50 vibrations of my own ruddy countenance before
the grand lens refocused itself—I walked beneath
the dirtiest of oaks, the nuttiest of silver clouds.
People should play coital instead of playing coy.
(Who was that Barbara Streisand character? Coit'l?)
How does the eye slip a button through a buttonhole?
How does the eye unzip the zipper, tooth by tooth?
A nudist can be undressed twice, same as you & you.
There are two tempers to each person; both are bare.

L=A=N=G=U=I=S=H Poetry

So, a guy walks into a bar along with a huge growling grizzly, and the maître d hollers, "Oh my god! Table for two?" and the guy replies: "Thanks. I know this grizzly situation may be difficult— *bear with me*!"

Meanwhile, the insect had been dead for such a long time, rigor mantis had set-in, but more than that, it'd gotten fashionable to be a dead insect; it was de rigueur mantis.

I like to sit in the portion of the aircraft where ordinary passengers receive self-help lectures, you know, motivational coach.

A fellow once sat next to me in motivational coach, a famous baseball slugger traveling to attend a Jewish girl's coming of age ceremony.

He would be, in fact, Casey at the Bat Mitzvah.

The village crier scrambled into the town square in a state of alarm: "The Scot is dead," he shouted, "the Scot is dead."

"Oh no!" someone called back, "how'd he die?"

"He was kilt!"

In an unrelated development, an Irish pop-rock band had to fill out so much American employment paperwork, they changed their name to W2.

"No more leads," lamented the police detectives, as they chowed-down some lunch at a Mexican restaurant.

"Yep," they lamented, "it's a real cold case-a-dilla."

Das Lunchmeats

The rate of surplus value divided by a thirty-aught-six continued to result in Lunchmeats. There will be, Fellow Citizens, someday, a National Museum of the American Lunchmeats, which will feature papier-mâché replicas of submarine and other nautical sandwiches. According to the bloated blue mimeograph that the young worshipper relied upon for restroom reading, one should pray to one's guardian angel to help free daddy's skid steer loader from the water table. The cool dew lubricated the deep grass, and that's when the attentional difficulties came on, Religion, Venison, Religion, Venison, although reverence toward one typically resulted in plenty of the other. The neighbor threatened to power up his scraper box. Those were dime store, joke store antlers, they had been stapled to the buck's head, if only it were a buck, if only there were carbohydrates, then the opportunity for a bipartisan BBQ may have hokey-pokeyed. The Cosmonaut endured his epigastric difficulties because he re-galled the epigastric difficulties of his Cossack forebears and the types of Caucasic Distress they had overcome, and this exercise resulted in the type of Orbital Weightlessness never possible at Dairy Queen or during a snack chips felony. Lunchmeats is a reward system; though, in the wrong hands Lunchmeats can be a false summit. Consider the DSM-V Manual of psychiatric diagnoses: no. 823.09—Lunchmeats Disorder, Moderate. Symptoms include speaking to Lunchmeats in frank, rational tones, demanding to know what became of Youth. "Give me some answers," the sufferer can be heard to say, whilst harrying an English muffin. The hurricane remnants came through for half an hour. The worshipper's daddy and the neighbor stood there, hands on hips, lamenting how hurricane remnants whuddn't what they used to be. The neighbor powered up his scraper box. The game animal came out of the woods, then—shoot, it could've been the Duchesser Windsor, but it was Fourth and 2, and Coach was sending out the taxi squad, or so said the Television Set, Religion, Venison, Religion, Venison.

Beef Pineapple Robot

I have become the kind of person who can order biscuits over gravy but not the kind of person who can tolerate the true definition of a Constitutional—what is, essentially, bicycle chaos. The French grape suffers more than the Chilean grape and more than the Syrian grape, but does it suffer more than the Russian potato? The Walloons ballooned and the Huguenots tied themselves into Huge Knots. People say that they are Walloons. Do people say that they are Walloons? People say that they are Flemish, after all, as well as Phlegmish. Newspaper titles need to be more flexible. *The North County Times*, for instance, really should be recast as *The North County Good & Bad Times*. Whatever the case may be, Southern California has a higher percentage of Experimental Yogis than any other region on the globe. Speaking of which—said Yogis have much to say on the topics of globulization and Globular Warming. Meat eaters may swallow the fear of the animal, but that doesn't mean the meat eaters shall become fearful; in fact, it means that they will become Chicken Satay Robot. Some will become Drunken Noodle Robot while others will become Beef Pineapple Robot. There is no Moo Shu Pork Robot although there is Moo Shu Porkbarrel Robot and his name is Congress. After Tex / Mexy, I was Lava / Tory and then I felt human again, i.e., I could, once again, Go for the Jugular or is that Go for the Juggler? The Sea Breeze came face to face with the Santa Ana and the result was When Microclimates Collide. A cute angle is obtuse; when you dream it, all angles are gifts, yours is I Sauce a Lease—Eye Saws the Police—Applesauce Please, dig it and "ridic" as in Ridiculous, Citizen, as in the Walloonie Bin.

Demographics

Notice how Stoic Muttons always stand to the right no matter where the camera is placed. You can say PRIME-er or PRIM-er, whichever. You can say inseam, or you can say *trompe l'oeil*. There may be a white boy with a thumbtack or a black boy in the hedge. You may decide to hate artists or, to be safe, you may decide to hate everyone. There is always some joker who cannot navigate a pool party, socially speaking, i.e., cheeseburgers, sun-tans, and gas-powder. "Arousal" and "The Scorpions" are mutually exclusive such that it is not possible to experience a modern arousal while hearing songs played by The Scorpions, an English-singing hair-metal combo from good old Germany, *ja ja, die rootin' tootin' und die wiener schnitzel*. If it were 1984, you'd be involved in drama outside the Pepperidge Farms store at the strip mall in the middle of the night. Lip gloss, a clash of foreheads, and a police action. Enjoli: "Unh." Enjoli: "Unh." Them's not no coincidence. Nope. Them's Demographics. Has anyone ever, at any time, said, "Fisticuffs in the Urals?" or "Buttocks on the Andes?" or "Liposuction beside the Himalayas?" Some Turks battle turds while other Turks battle Kurds. There are Products for what ails you and, then again, there are no Products for what ails you. The results, in the end, stupefy even the brightest bulbs in the garden. The world does not come in stereo, unless you happen to live nearby a disaster. To wit, there were once pay phones, antennae, and sit-down meals. Every citizen had a snake story. To deconstruct was to slap one's self with another person's hand. "Chug, chug, chug," many used to shout. Planets are no better than junkies. There is Want and there is Must. Which best defines you?

To Kick a Mockingbird's Ass

Days ago, during a muggy jog up towards the Cathedral, a mockingbird assaulted me in front of the Australian Embassy, while a uniformed Secret Service officer ate a submarine sandwich. He proceeded to alight in a distant oak and did what mockingbirds do; he mocked me. He discussed the importance of swing voters in the presidential race, he spoke to me in rusty French, he submitted some poems for publication. He didn't say etcetera. He said, "Recession." He said, "Try pissing into a dixie cup during a Category Five Twister." Then his song faded. A mockingbird could certainly best a Finch, even one that nested in the Atticus. Still, I agree with Harper Lee in noting that a mockingbird should not be killed. We should kick its ass, instead. If only we could confront the thug where he alights. O, Lord: Why is there perch? There is perch, sayeth the Lord, to remind us of what a serpent is not. Why is there serpent? There is serpent, sayeth the Lord, to administer justice. Justice? What does the serpent know of justice? It knoweth not, sayeth the Lord. That's the point. O, Lord: help me! Take a seasalt bath, sayeth the Lord. Engage in the utility of lavender. Lord: why didst thine mockingbird assault me? Mine mockingbird, sayeth the Lord, assaulteth even me, that pesky son of a gun, with those dilly wings and that dilly tail. Tis why I createth the hawk, but yesterday I didst espy the mockingbird routing the hawk. We must soaketh the brisket over-night, sayeth the Lord, then leave it beneath the distant oak, for the mockingbird dost judge our fate. Huzzah!

Labour Saving Devices

I've heard of people wanting to be Spanked but not always Lifted. Also note the Blindfold and (apparent) Electricity and (apparent) Distress. Good Gravy. What will we ask for next? To be Understood? To be Hiccoughed? Is there an Understanding and Hiccoughing Machine out there? Yesterday, in the unoccupied Fourth Floor Men's Room at the Institution where I work, an Automated Toilet flushed, and flushed, and flushed. What ghostly arse was haunting that toilet? What ghostly turd was that toilet flushing again and again, like Sissy-fuss? For eternity. Or, at least, for Wednesday. Maybe it's just the Advance Guard Toilet for Today's Busy Professional: "Always Ready for Your Ass." I bet there are some pregnant women out there who'd want a true Labour Saving Device, huh? Maybe even British politics needs a Labour Saving Device. Speaking of Brits, if Shakespeare lived today, he may very well have written *Papaya King* instead of *King Lear*. It would be a story about a man having to divide up his Hot Dog & Juice Empire among his daughters and, in the process, find True Love. In the end, all the characters don't die, exactly, but grow complacent due to all the Labour Saving Devices they own. It would be, thus, a uniquely American tragedy that would also involve Pizza Hut, Cable News, and dyspepsia. "It burns," King Papaya would say after eating an Oreo Pizza on the couch during election returns. "How now, Nuncle?" would say the Fool. "Dost thou have Heartburn or Acid Reflux Disease?" There ensues a pause. The pause is everything.

Études, Brute?

Julius Caesar suspects Brutus of practicing compositions on the piano. "I heard music," the strongman alleges. "Études, Brute?" If only our back-stabbiz had been musicians, instead. They'd of (sic) kept their steely, steely connives in their two-nix and we'd of (sic) slugged-down a Donald Duck à l'Orange Julius Caesar Salad. In short, weed'a lived and it wouldn'a been uh backstabbiz atoll. Later, Caesar and Brutus haggle over which catalogue-retailer to patronize. "J. Crew, Brute?" says Caesar. They have some thought-baboons in this arena, some Ideas of Merch. To this point, the pooch hasn't initiated a coup, a coo hasn't emanated from the putsch. And as for empire, Romulus hasn't reamed us out, Remus hasn't loaded a CD-Romulus into the disc drive. Anything could happen, even détente, even breaking bread, peace-meal. It's both terrifying and wonderful all at once, kind of like Brutus bored out of his bust, making his late-night Bru-tay call to a gal, a Gaul pursued by the scent-o'tour himself. Rife goes on. A gambling conference kindles-up at a hotel across the street where someone delivers The Keno Address. When indentured servants reinsert their false teeth, they become dentured servants, no? Ever notice how antlers resemble driftwood? It's like mature bucks are washing up on shore, waves and waves of sea-sawbucks, them and their weather-worn driftwood antlers, ten bucks a dozen in Ten-buck-two. If you have a job, or if you seek a job, then you're under occupation. At the request of Brutus, Julius Caesar agrees to engage in the nautical guessing game, Battleship. "A-2, Brute?" he guesses. He guesses correctly, even though he doesn't kitchen-sink no gravy bloat. The bodies of the other senators reflect on every bright surface, their motions unlike stabbing but in emphasis of their numbers, their jagged rationale. They attack Julius Caesar for being a crass-dressing tyranny even as they, themselves, will become tyranny, with or without the salad dressage, and they, themselves, will be slain by the residents of tyranny 2-B. Recital is a good deity, too shrewd for the mothball operas that resolve themselves (phone booth, no mouthpiece) in the public confessionals of prepaid gravity amid the sunlit metals of confrontation.

Pollstergeist

pollstergeist

Noun | Poll · ster · geist | / ˈpōl-stər-ˈgīst /

: A spirit that disrupts questions for a political poll, the tallies of a poll, the presentation of a poll, and the effects of a poll in determining the outcome of an election.

Examples of pollstergeist in sentences:

1. The pollstergeist replied "Hillary" every time the pollster asked a voter for his or her preference in the election, thereby leading experts to conclude that Clinton would defeat Trump.

2. The Democrats were toppled when a pollstergeist spread misinformation during the 2016 presidential contest, the results from which caused the party's relevance to fluctuate.

First definitive use of pollstergeist: November 9, 2016.

Synonyms: Ouija Wedgie, Seer Sucker, Tedium Rare

Antonyms: Chekhov, Scalia, van Leeuwenhoek

Word origin: Pal (Dutch, chum) Stir (Old English, porridge manipulation), Gas (Greek, flatus).

Variation:

poultrygeist: A haunted chicken. A cage-free, pasture-raised, foraging, haunted chicken that lays deviled eggs. Eating the eggs will increase your revenant cholesterol. Sucking on the eggs will mimic the recent anguish of Democrats [n.b. Not to be confused with poultryheist (grand theft chicken.)]

Interview with a Yes Man

The earth weathers numerous isometrics of sexual rejection.

Who delivered this pulpy cantaloupe or, if you will, this melon of dubious fragrance?

Even the strongest radio channel flirts with the jagged frontiers of static; every exposure must penetrate the scrim.

The cold, quiet synapse-spaces that once conducted pain—as music—to the hemisphere.

Either the tree or the man might grow crookedly, the man rooted among the poverty of other crooked trunks.

A project dubbed "Move the Hillside" indeed moved the hillside to a secondary location dubbed "Secondary Hillside."

The number of rusty vehicles the number of dormant vehicles the rusty dormant corner of town.

Light presides the percentage of light presiding the percent of impotent radiation.

Where ample sustenance coincides with the outcry for sustenance: reveal, to me, this arena.

Animals that would never contact one another assembled in the same sandwich, every day, in every city.

Oh, there are deer but no woods; the deer idle on the outskirts.

A moment of astonishment before brute force, brutes applying tourniquets, et cetera, prevails.

Will the world evict us? Will you think about my hands?

The greater distinction hinges on saying Yes.

For Dissidence

We are full of anger and decency—the anger of a fragile cliff
and the decency of a broken lock: the circularity of its numerical
loneliness. Consider the percentage of news that arrives staticky

over walkie talkies. A fact happened. I say "eek!" Jokingly!
How the hell do you say "eek!" *The eek shall inherit the earth*?
It's raining on the four track northbound beside the smokestack,

top of which grows a flowering-forth, deciduous beauty; these
bouquets at the end of the barrel tend to mimic the joke pistols
and underwhelming crowns of fireworks that accompany

our narrow-gauge politics. It's raining on the freight tracks near
Baltimore, outrageous stocky drops, the mineral concept of dollar
coins. A departure bell snaps around like (grayscale) whirlybird

fingertips in lenitive wind. Later, the smudge of the moon
playing above a ruckus of revivalist chairs arriving, or an upward
smudge of moon playing above the ruckus of chairs packed off

for a secondary destination. What, therefore, cannot be
enumerated? The reputable wavelengths of distal objects?
Here swerves the leaf-like trajectory of a bonny idea, forgotten,

the years-in-relevance of a lifespan or redemption-as-industry
despite witnesses. A sweaty, bloated special prosecutor arrives.
He receives one (1) perfunctory office in the basement beside

the Feudalist, one (1) stack of official documents, differing
from that of the Feudalist, and one (1) forehead-mounted
flashlight to enable the myopic scrutiny of fissures and cleavages.

In time, the Feudalist will embezzle the special prosecutor's
nickel-plated cigar-pinching device. All citizens shall be classified
"essential personnel" and, as such, issued signage that reads

"Break out of the cycle good" and "Break out of the cycle bad."
American deer, in particular, will offer stern topographies
of the weather: doe as hotfoot pelt, aggressive juvenile buck

but for the branch bristling, the leaves bright with seasonal dew,
the shrink-wrap woods. Strip malls adjoin every America,
especially districts that foretell a quilt-work of occasional

calamity. The halo of a drive-thru! All these worlds natural,
the heaped-up galaxies gleaming amid the despondent wisdom
of coherence. (*Too many luxury automobiles rotate like cakes*

in glassy buildings.) Man weighs his deficits on the greengrocer's scale. I'm so stunned—wordplays flail me. I should aspire to be more than a kindly fellow occupying the meritorious space

at the denouement of a crisis, sporting hoodlum attire with "you betcha" nonchalance. No, let's consider the pastels
of soft spoken resistance, many such kingdoms, borderless…

Essay after Another Episode of Angry Prejudice

Some people read poems about spending time in graveyards.
They don't hate these poems. "Ooh!" they say.
"I *hate* spending a lot of *time* in *graveyards*."
Not all poems are about loitering in cemeteries, though.

Some lyrics concern a horsey, the current president,
or the prevalence of vulgarity. "Vulgarity-current president,"
says one ambitious verse. "Horsey-vulgarity," goes another.
Yet a third may offer, "Current president-horsey."

If someone died, there follows the day after someone died.
That day is almost always wintry,
even if it's the chalky cloud-swells of a wintry sky
during a season of oppressive heat.

Can the sky grow any oilier or smokier? In the end,
there are no achievable geometries. (Can you disprove it?)
Perhaps the word "achievable" should be subtracted.
It supposes attainment, as in scaling a truth,

or encountering a love that forever regenerates forgiveness.
Another person has been slain. Most cessation doesn't murder,

but murder almost always results in cessation.
Perhaps the holy nature of stoppages kindles an impulse

to envision the kingdom of the dead.
Of all the unachievable geometries—wandering,
sound maps, savage proximity, slackening—only slackening
results in catastrophe. There follows the day after someone died.

That day, and every day in succession, is a white stone.
Can you disprove it?
My friend, we're *all* going to spend a lot of *time* in *graveyards*.
Ever notice how walking is like the body through the body?

Currency jangles in a coin pocket.
The afternoon declares shady intervals
until the curvature and curtain of disengagement.
Some people read poems about the moon,

its quarter-hopes and half-hopes, its hidden alertness.
They don't hate these poems. The moon tugs
and we may listen, in order to defamiliarize.
As with any loss, how crucial the disbelief?

Prayer for a Former Student Who Clings to Life in an Unknown Hospital

The word of your name returns as echo.
It is my voice but watery, heavy with final syllable.
The sound skips across the rain-dark plane of the afternoon.

An echo can originate anywhere: valley, wall,
person, recollection, theory, guesswork.
One must traverse-try; one must envision the striking-surface.

Will I grow expert in the forlorn art?
The object receives the skill of the inquiry.
The cleaner the return, the closer the object.

But proximity may be a map, the coordinates where echo
may originate, in minutes and seconds.
Proximity might be painful, but echo requires neighborhood.

If I am to find you, I must suffer through
the possibility of shape bent-against blurry color.
(Imprecise, me.)

What is echolalia? Echo et alia?
As if there were echo + echoes,
which confounds the mission to discover.

The inquiry at a remove; jangle of clashing voices + directions.
If the echo never varies.
The same stolid note, a clatter in place of language.

An echo becomes a bird. An echo becomes a bird
climbing through the echo of mistranslation.
A realtor might say: "Echolocation! Echolocation! Echolocation!"

I imagine you finding this witty, whatever your state.
Laughter, I realize, might disarray the apparatus that sustains you.
Lightning hacks through air toward a tree.

The very same splintering noise, a limb separating from the tree.
At once, lightning and the heavy wood tearing from its trunk.
What I mean is, I am trying to locate you.

Many years ago, I concluded a poem by writing
[that I] try to catch echoes with my hands.
At last, I know what these words mean. I will persevere.

Teaching the Cannon

Imagine a world in which you're no longer a Professor of Literature teaching the canon, but a Professor of Cannon teaching the cannon. You realize that more sophisticated methods of delivering ordnance have arrived on the battlefield (and on the briny) (and in the cobalt, cobalt sky) yet you believe in a simpler, more classical war. "These implements," you lecture, "might become requisite again, given the many catastrophes that may befall humankind, returning us to a more primitive, and enthralling, imposition of will." A proper Professor of Cannon should teach the architecture of the device—the solid spaces and the negative—as well as the intellectual aspects of field artillery. Angle of fire and rate of fire, to be sure, but also the type of spark and type of propellant that ultimately lob the ball toward the fortifications. Your specialty, "Collateral Damage," has yet to become unfashionable: the howling cannon-fire gone astray, and the ensuing despair of the unintended targets. Every so often, you congratulate yourself on completing a dissertation in this area, as this specialty provides you with a renewable means of presenting papers at conferences and pursuing promotions at your institution. "Fire!" you shout at your students. On cue, each of your students takes a turn shouting "Fire!" at the blackboard, where you've sketched out replica lip, muzzle, neck, and all the rest. As a special treat, you surprise your classes by playing the R.E.M. song, "The One I Love," in which the singer croons, "Fire," every so often. A very postmodern debate ensues about the intent of such a lyric; some students argue that Michael Stipe must've been kindling a fuse a couple paces behind the chamber, so to speak, of a modern artillery piece, and yet other students contend that the song, "The One I Love," belongs in another can(n)on altogether, the meaning of which troubles you, haunts your sensibilities. Perhaps you repair to the comfortable trappings of your office with a takeaway mug of decaf, noodling around in a canonical way: filing cabinet, bookshelf, computer, window, armchair. You relish the thought that, next semester, you will be on sabbatical, rising when you wish and working when you wish, if working means to grind coffee and peruse the Sunday funnies. In your absence, you realize, your students may be taught a thoroughly different cannon, but of course you, too, could consider teaching another cannon—or rather no canon, at all.

The Doctrine Is IN.

"I smell errata!"
or so sayeth the Cosa Nostradamus.

Takeout Bakeout

Say "Drugs" to "No" and "Narcotics" to "Nah"
and "Dope" to "Nope." What time you got?
The time is Now. We cannot, as a Society, separate.
We cannot separate (the) State from Salt,
(the) Lick from Bone, (the) Dry from Park,
(the) Avenue from Light, (the) House from God,
and so forth. Can you batch? we know you can botch,
can you butcher, as in slaw? can you dozen the alternatives?
can you batch? Can you bundle? we know you can bandy,
can you bindle, as in slaw? can you dozen the alternatives?
can you clump? What time you got at Five past Five?
To empower the Trick Question, please press "1"
on your Rotary Phone. Beware, though.
The empowered Trick Question may ask you,
trick you, task you, ask. An empowered Trick Question,
par example, once interrogated an entire office full of
Fraud Investigators, investors, gators, and Frauds,
with some slippery Freudian trickery:
What time you got at Five past Five?
Can you knot? we know you can knit, can you gnat,
as in slaw? can you dozen the alternatives, can you batch?
Say "Narcotics" to "Nah" and "Dope" to "Nope."
If you can separate, and if you can separate,
please press "1" on your rotary phone.

Consider Tense When Observing a Horse

A sawhorse in the past or a sea horse in the present.
It's rehearsal if you practice a play in advance,
not another trip in a hearse unless,
of course, the play struggles.
Hirsute, on the other hand, doesn't refer to her outfit,
it's not her suit, or her strong suit,
but she sure might wear the hair-shirt.
All the boxers I don't know—all the other breeds I don't know—
I can't be debriefed on boxers. I can't write a pugilist—
I can't write a to-do list—I can't write an evangelist.
Even Jell-O could sate an evangelical,
or maybe the effect would be intangible:
is there a tangelo, aye, in the punch?
I can, you can, he she it cans, we canned,
you canned, they canned heat, answers, tomatoes.
Ghengis Khan Job, Ghengis Cannes Job,
Ghengis Cannes Edison, Ghengis Khan Carne.
The biblical hard luck case Jōb, okay? Okay.
Biblical Jōb Description, Biblical Jōb Market,
Biblical Hand Jōb, Biblical Book of Blow Jōb,
the Biblical Book of Jōb Search, Jōb Loss.
A hearse is a hearse of course of course unless it's Mr. Dead.

List of Rejected Conspiracy Theories

If it's feasible, then it can be stored in the freezer.
If it's dirigible, then it can be mourned by a dirge.
Too many dirges, however,
might cause you to walk with a blimp.
In the next room, Yokel Ono sits on a barstool
and croons about life in the rural prefecture.
In one of the songs, an ante-lope makes off with the poker kitty
that otherwise belongs to the rubber baron. He, the rubber baron,
derives great affluence from prophylactic sales,
but his business practices draw wide condom-nation.
So yeah, a different fellow wants to raise fruit trees in anonymity
and adopts a *nom de plum*, or would that be a *nom de prune*?
Sadly, he struggles at agriculture and succumbs,
mildly, to gardening of the arteries.
His real name is Norman; he's a standard fellow,
and when war finally erupts, he settles on *Norm de Guerre*
as the assumed name for his saboteur of duty.
Eventually, his alias gets him on the A-List.
When the Jerusalemite studies you, by the by,
he got his Zion you, he got his eye on you.
I hate it when the hit man, Mr. Reaper Cussin's,
mouths off, over and over. Finally, I confront the hit man,
Mr. Reaper Cussin's. "Hey Bud," I say. "Are you assassin' me?"

Interview with a Volunteer Who Just Wants to Give Back to the Community

Where is the Look Sea?
Is that around here?
I don't remember a lake of that name.
Oh, what are people talking about?
That guy at the Rec Center was full of it!
Carrying on about the "Invisigoths." Pfff.
All the Goths I know are visible.
The gals—in their black lipstick?
Hey, wait a minute: Is it KFC-Wendy's
or BK-Taco Bell or IHOP-HoJo?
My physician said, "Keep up your lifestyle
& you'll wind up w/ a long hitch in
Sciatica Prison—w/o payroll."
That is *not* primary care.

Preponderances

Confuse "Tunnel" for "Night" as you would
(2) Curvature for Curvaceous;
(3) Concavity for Concave;
(4) Likeness for Like;

(5) Sooty-black for Star-black;
(6) Segment for Segment + remainder;
(7) Entries for Preponderances;
(8) The Lost Age for The Likely Outcome.

Confuse "Tunnel" for "Night" as you would
(10) Affront for Inelasticity;
(11) The Chord of the Solo for The Arc;
(12) Adumbration for Completion + shock.

But please don't mistake "A Ledge of Clarity"
for (14) The Way You Could Be Loved: (*don't.*)

Fourteen Periods (for Clarice Lispector)

A young woman walked against the traffic, downhill, the breezy orbit of her scarf—the swept springs—uncovering her, a sonorous swerve, ringlets brunette, varnished at street corners in the dipping light of eye contact. The many dress heels to pavement, the minutes and halves of a percussion compass would offer a bliss-erratic as bright as the tours of flickers, but for the directional mechanism of depletions in reverse. Those drab-dressed, vents whipping or other exodus, the day flattening. Three months later plus an hour, the weather had returned to seasonal: granular tableau above the river's widening, husk yellow.

She repaired, at the river, to the gradations of a hill, clean grass and dusty crown overlooking an eddy revolving with one styrofoam cup. Trees across the water in woolens. The sky lofted towards the coordinates of digital transmission. To receive alloys, the sub-frigid metals of static, the needle electric in the ear, despair, of the listener.

An air traffic pattern was changing, a rope of departures growling at the dimming detonation of the west. "I would shrink from attackers," she may have thought. The young woman would turn away from the laugh of a bottle-thrower breaking, perhaps, on a vacant basketball court. An open palm, she concluded, is not always grasping for a handout, but a device that measures risk. The skeptic. The skeptic.

What's Comin' Atcha

[1]

Oh, great. The Extroverts are coming. "The Extroverts are coming." They brought their friends, too: some Extra-verts. Now you'll have to perform the entire suite of difficult handshakes: the clap, the hug, and the snap. With everyone! Here come the two Joes: Slappy Joe and Sloppy Joe. "Where's Joe?" someone says. "I dunno," says Slappy Joe. "You seen him?" says Slappy Joe. "Nah," says Sloppy Joe. "I ain't seen him." It starts to rain, a sloppy rain. It starts to wind, a slappy wind. We go to the basement, to the Coffers, but discover, much to our chagrin, all the Coughers have been locked in the Coffers. It's a Coffers fulla Coughers. Boy, are they relieved to see us. A clock that can't tell time ... has a tick disorder.

[2]

A bear chases a Russian man up a tree. "Nyet!" shouts the man, but the bear knows the difference between "Nyet!" and a Kalashnikov. "Nyet!" shouts the Russian as the bear climbs the tree. Perchance the bear shall turn on you someday, which is a good reason to avoid Russia altogether. If you had to choose between the clippiz (sic) and the tweeziz (sic), which would you choose? One will buzz while the other will pluck. When your choices are getting (a) buzzed or (b) plucked—I suppose your choices ain't half bad. The mockingbird swoops, of course, but the raptor is comin' atcha, too. The gung-ho osprey swoops. It is so gung-ho, this osprey, it has maximum *osprey de corps*.

[3]

Your order arrives. An optimistic helping of waffle with blueberry "compote" on a big round plate: it arrives. "Compote," you think. "Isn't that a pile of junk in the corner of the garden?" Huh. Now it's on your waffle. You sit down and decide to self-radicalize. The time has come. Every other attempt at self-radicalization (blueberry compote, etc.) hasn't yielded much in the way of radical behavior. You notice a box of inflammatory literature on the front stoop with a sign that reads, "Free Radical." So long as you're moving forward, the back of your head is—comin' atcha! Scams and plausible deceptions may appear, but a few good words persevere. If you're still reading this—and I hope you are—it means that I love you. So? ... Make me an offer.

Under Armoire

I've got so many athletic commitments—such as clubbing and jumbo slice—that I've accumulated numerous pieces of athletic underwear to the tune of closet-busting. You might imagine boxer-jocks dangling importantly from marquee hangers amid my notable suite of salmon-tint Casual Day home kits. So I upped the antechamber. For all my Under Armour, I bought an Under Armoire. Did you know about this? It has room for sporty sock, sporty pant, sporty tote, sporty sideways cap. (I store my sporty cap sideways, in any event, to get it broken in-for athletic commitments such as clubbing and jumbo slice.) I thought it would end there, and by "it" I mean the accumulation of athletic underwear, and by "there," I mean my Under Armoire, but Nö, I begin to desire greater domination, the way Under Armour conquered the body, one garment at a time. I would like to own an Under Armoured Car and travel the Land Down Under Armour, not to mention purchase shares in the corporate merger that will certainly produce Under Armour & Hammer. I could see this getting way outta hand. If I max my credit cards, what then? Must I appear in Debtors Court? Will my wages get garnished? Will they hand me my money with a sprig of parsley? All because of my insatiable requirement to fill my drawers—with drawers!

Rimbaud: First Blood

Sylvester Stallone stars as Rambo in *Rimbaud: Première Sang*, an action-adventure film in which a young French poet escapes persecution by literary critics and avenges this persecution with surreal verse. "Yo, Verlaine!" says Stallone as Rambo as Rimbaud. "They drew first blood, not me!" Verlaine, played by Bruce Willis, sits in a hovel with Rambo as Rimbaud, having helped Rimbaud elude water cannon and the poetry canon. On the one hand, Willis plays Verlaine, but on the other hand, Stallone plays Rambo playing Rimbaud. The production crew can't automatically compute where Stallone ends and where Rambo begins, where Rambo ends and Rimbaud begins. One scene, a bromance entitled "Ram-bro," calls for a passionate fist-bump between Rambo as Rimbaud and Willis as Verlaine. Afterwards, Stallone and Willis compare their future engagements. Willis will appear as a Jewish wine merchant in a TV series entitled *Chico and the Manischewitz*. Stallone will appear on a rival network—as a fellow who suffers from gynecomastia—in *Chico and the Man Boobs*. "Yo, Verlaine!" cries Stallone as Rambo as Rimbaud, but the camera shows the viewer that Willis has departed. Rambo as Rimbaud holds a battered sheet of onionskin to his face. The camera shows a dirty, sweaty, camouflaged man reading verse. He is Rambo one minute, he is Rimbaud another minute, he is a real laughing hiatus.

Postmodern Tentacle Liturgy

He who spends too much time focused on Tentacle is a sucker, Gran'daddy always used to say. More and more Tentacle washing ashore each morning, though, cause of Al Gore. Tent plus pinnacle = the nipple of the octopus. A man squeezes a woman's nipple, a woman squeezes a man's nipple, only amongst primates. Go ahead, but if you pinch octopus nipple you will be in a world of suction. Don't forget to catch Antique Tentacle Roadshow and play that game "Disappointed" / "Not Disappointed" when Tentacle is evaluated by Postmodern Paddle Wackers. Some folks think they have antique Tentacle and are disappointed when the appraisal is low, whereas some people think they have modest Tentacle when it turns out they have very valuable Tentacle, and are elated, to say the least. The same Tentacle—chopped high and chopped low—has sat in the Thai Knot sushi prep area for years, rotated every so often by a sushi chef in a white mushroom cap. That's how Tentacle matures. Unless it's bottled and Put Up. I wouldn't turn down a bottle of Tentacle 12 Year Single Brine, but that's me. A tired octopus is a Spentacle, whereas a gladiator cephalopod is a Spartacus. The Mongols, when they ran out of Tentacle, would catapult their own slain comrades—especially those festering with the bubonic death—into the citadels of their enemies. "Incoming Tentacle!" the sentries would shout at first, until they saw a dead Mongol fly into their camp. "Incoming!" they would shout instead, or "Mongol!" until it became commonplace, all those Besiegers flying through the air, and the sentries quit shouting, quit their posts, quit the citadels, but failed to notify their adversaries, who kept launching their mates in broad arcs.

Sugar in the Raw

Let's face it: we can control our climate
but not our primate. Adulterers are those
who criminally impersonate adults.
I send you my (r)egrets because
I'd rather you be visited by a seafowl.
Depressed about protocol?
Take your antideprecedents.
The British have it right: their raincoats,
the way they talk. The Scot took a *doomp*.
A brick layer is a mason in the trowel-wielding sense,
that is, one who specializes in the "escapades"
and ice capades of sunbaked or kiln-fired clay products.
Perversely, a marine layer is not an individual
who specializes in the urges of our fighting men
but a cloud pattern blown ashore from the sea,
the holey see. To be swayed by suede
is to stand in deference to indifference.
A summands is a noun; derives from summa;
a term in a summation. An addenda to an agenda.
What kind of society debates free condoms
when it won't offer free condiments?
Us and our low carburetor diets.
Our liens and our leotards. Our chains and our neo-chards.
God Bless the Good Ol' United States of Corporation. Lo Mein!

OfayCupid

"Oh, why go on?" said the traveler,
after arriving in a dry county: "it's pint-less." Outside,
actors and actresses reenacted *Gunfight at the Ofay Corral.*
Afterwards, they cruised each other at OfayCupid.
All this online dating necessitates the return of the dative case;
it's all so indirect. I put down one summer read
for another summer read, *A Passage to Indianapolis*
for *The Unbearable Lightness of Bee Sting.*
I put down *The Unbearable Lightness of Bee Sting*
for *Topic of Capricorny*. Do you put down books?
It's very insulting. Samuel Butler may know *The Way of All Flesh,*
whereas most modern toilets know the way of all flush.
At the very end of the flush resides a ferocious reptile—
a Commode O'dragon. His dream dessert?
A slice of pie a la commode. Did a state of despair—
pointlessness—facilitate the painting technique,
pointillism? By acknowledging all the pints, indeed,
one can contemplate The Big Tincture.

Interview with a Child in Time Out

Dad says that Time Out is punishment but on TV
when a coach calls Time Out the players hug &
the scrubs run onto the court for, like, 30 seconds
I declare this to Dad then he sends me into Time Out
now I have to stand near the record player where Dad
has propped up an album called *Time Out*—ha ha—
very funny—by a guy named Dave Brubeck Quartet
Dad closes his eyes & gets all rubbery when he plays it
& when he plays *Time Out*, Mom gets all rubbery, too
I try to get rubbery like Mom & Dad—to be a family—
but Dad sends me into Time Out w/ no rubbery option
so I try to think deep thoughts, you know, like should I
dookie in the peepee toilet at school & show everyone &
it must look like I'm practicing in Time Out b/c uh oh!

On Sensitivity: A Brief History of Political Choice

The dentist prepared to drill my tooth without any anesthetic. He said, "Raise your left hand if you feel any sensitivity" but I'm like "Why the left—because I'm a *liberal*?" but he's like "Hey, *I'm* from Brooklyn!" so I said, "If I raise my left hand due to sensitivity, will you raise your left hand to acknowledge my sensitivity?" We tested it out once, in the absence of sensitivity, me raising my left hand, he raising his left hand, but in the end it wasn't the moment I'd hoped for—you know, a camaraderie amongst everyday people in my life: train conductors, specialized personnel, troubleshooters, certificate holders, dentists, et cetera. He continued to drill my tooth without anesthetic, so I got to thinking about sensitivity. Am I too sensitive? Are we Americans too sensitive? How many people, at the moment, are raising their left hands due to sensitivity? *Shoot*: how many people, at the moment, are raising their *right* hands due to sensitivity? Isn't that the crux of the political problem we face? If more Americans raise their left hands than their right hands, then maybe we could elect the sensitive guy. A small piece of metal sprang into the back of my mouth, but the dentist plucked it out, deftly. "Thanks for not swallowing *that*!" he said. He sat down and took off his mask. "It's all over," he added. "You didn't need any anesthesia." He stared at the far dentistry horizon. I said, "That's a good thing, right? Not needing anesthesia." Because we could raise any hands we wanted. Or better yet, we could raise no hands at all.

Oh, There Are Hearts

The Boy with the Broken Heart and the Boy with the Overflowing Heart sit, tables apart, at the Howard Johnson Breakfast Buffet. You can tell who's who by noting which of the two presides over a plate heaping with home fries and ketchup and which of the two presides over a plate of melon cubes and yoghurt. You can tell who's who by noting which of the two has groomed himself a fancy facial hair display and which of the two has allowed his facial hairs to grow unkempt like a weedy lea. There are girls, oh, there are girls. There are hopes, oh, there are hopes. There is bacon, oh, there is bacon. And there are Hearts, oh, there are Hearts. One of these Hearts is Broken and one of these Hearts is Overflowing. The two Boys write poems. They write sheathes of poems. In one of the sheathes, the Heart Overflows. In the other sheath, the Heart Breaks. Perhaps you can guess which of the two Boys wrote which of the two sheathes. Things tend to correspond—to correlate—to arrange themselves for devotion—in these ways.

The Boy with the Broken Heart wins the Pulitzer Prize. Well, not yet, but many years from now, his Collected Sheathes will triumph. He will be easy to spot in a crowd. He will sit in an armchair surrounded by Boys and Girls who wear goatees on their chins and flowers in their hair, respectively. "Whipped cream," he will say, and "My time in Venice," and "Grotesque dreams." Those sitting about him will say, "Ohhh." The Boy with the Broken Heart will be awarded an Endowed Chair at a Prestigious State University. It will be called the Broken Heart Endowed Chair in the Literary Art of Poetry Sheathing, and all will be well in the House of Babel, as they say in the song. But what of the Boy with the Overflowing Heart? He grows bitter. In his opinion, those who advance in the world of poetry sheathing say the word "F**k" too often and curse the current president. There are no chairs for him, poor soul, 'cept the ones at HoJo's. As a linguist would say: "There is a morale to this story." There is another kind of Heart out there. There are many such alternatives. Cultivate one of them. Then sing your F**king song.

Everything's a Burger

If you "Ain't Talkin' 'Bout Love" then what're you talkin' 'bout, just bein' friends? That's a burger. Van Halen's a burger. Similarly, if you "Feel Like Making Love" then you're not really making love, you're just feeling like it. (Who *doesn't*?) (Who doesn't *feel* like making love?) That's a burger. Bad Company's a burger.

What kind of music does a financial instrument play? Songs about executive salaries built upon the manipulation of your debt, that's what. I smell a burger. The guys from Accounting head to lunch. "I don't want a burger," they say, but they order fish 'n' chips / chips 'n' salsa. That's a burger. Alternative to burger's a burger.

This entrée was invented out of necessity many years ago in Europe by a class of people known as the Burghers. They lived in burghs (e.g., Pittsburghers) and they were busy, so they required a convenient repast. A chain sprung up, Burgher King, run by Old MacDonald. You've heard of him. He had a Firm, C-E, C-E-O.

"Duck Duck Goose" is a burger. Might as well stop calling for Red Rover and, instead, send burger right over. This land *is* both your land and my land *because* it's a burger. Fifty strip-malls, fifty strip-clubs, fifty strip-searches, fifty strip-mines sewn into the little square on the flag. Pledge allegiance to the burger, citizen.

Your alarm clock wakes you, is a burger. (Explanation: time's a burger.) You lie under the covers listening to the news, is a burger. (Radio's a burger.) You miss the express, and as a consequence, you miss your crucial meeting, is a burger. (Sloth's a burger.) Somewhere in the city wafts arena rock. Wafts the burger . . .

Blue Jay-Z

In order to really succeed, I'm prepping a cheesy resume,
my curriculum velveetae. I'll send it by Greek tragedy post,
via Medea Mail. The sunset prayer for scooter, Vespa's Vespers,
can be recited along with an affirmation of the Cuban highball,
c.f., "I got my mojito workin'!" Those who are rockin' the Casbah
versus those who are rockin' the cash bar: ask the coroner
down on the corner, drinking a Corona. By saying
"the Bohemian poet in *wetter* weather," do you mean
Rainier Maria Rilke? A maudlin passerine (blue jay)
considered simultaneously with the female republic (va-jay-jay)
considered simultaneously with *Reasonable Doubt* rapper (Jay Z)
yields one Blue Va-Jay-Jay Z. His unreleased masterpiece,
"Boner's Manual," (in lieu of traditional instructions),
should be distributed to every adolescent. If you want to know,
the French military always assigns a comedian to watch
the fuel depot in the desert, since the petrol patrol is drôle.
"Que Sahara Sahara," concludes the musketeer. Last I heard,
the pedestrian lady was marrying her traffic policeman;
oh yeah, she was wedding her whistle. After a wedding in Italy,
c.f., Roman nuptials, the couple will exchange views
of each other's sticky butts: a honey-moon. If a lettuce
could tell time, uh huh, it'd probably feature romaine numerals.
The drink mix Tang comes in many flavors: passionfruit,
guava, pineapple, so why not prune? Why not prune Tang?

Ineffable

To say "evening" as if the darkness settles scores.
Don't deny yourself mythology
on account of city planners and their poverty of ideas.
Don't deny yourself mythology.

If there is disassembly, then there might be calibration.
If there is no calibration, then our streets
will be mobbed with clock parts: hands, numerals,
gears, mechanisms, bejeweled recollections.

A resale shop that specializes in clock parts:
call it Secondhand Second Hand.
A used clock becomes your favorite timepiece.
Secondhand time becomes your favorite kind of time.

Ineffable, as in "Can't be F'ed up." How about ineffable?
The chilly clouds draped like Spanish moss
among the appalling textures of trees,
the allocation of dehydrated trees.

Or the cloud patterns resemble
the tectonic impatience of momentary continents.
The rain cycles through periods of building
and periods of idling. Thus, the rain forever.

Shuffle your feet if you desire panorama.
Every panorama differs, every shuffle varies.
Desk lamps burning in dark offices,
an entire corridor brightened in this dark way.

Boot sock, boot sock, out of doors.
Boot sock, boot sock, nobody knows this little grief
you bear. Boot sock, boot sock, out of doors.
Boot sock, boot sock, nobody knows you.

Moments De-installed from Servitude

The gloomy liberal and the crabby liberal pursue severe doctrine.
Both suckle a cage-free, pasture-raised hoompty doompty.
Allow the word "haunt." It's a looker's word.
Allow, allow, allow, allow, allow.
The sun bulges through a puncture.
Body temperature climbs another tenth, enjoyable.
Again, condensation overcomes the hierarchies of disorientation.
The gutters of mysterious syllables muddle
the bootblack echoes of central thoroughfare. [Consider:
moments de-installed from servitude, untethered
mechanisms that meter (1) inference or
(2) deduction.] As to the affiliations of reanimated cruelty?
A bullet rends the corners of a woman's impoverished overcoat,
the gray corners of her mouth an "O" of perpetual outrage.

People Who Don't Listen to Music

People who don't listen to music
park their cars in front of fire hydrants.
People who don't listen to music
develop repetitive stress disorders,
such as Dyspeptic Political Identity.
People who don't listen to music
lament the idle swells of "steely gray clouds"
dimming the north-northwest.
They wander through the lobby
in search of the lobby.
They perch like slumbering owls,
one-legged, on marble staircases.
They marvel at the defunct telephone booth,
the handset dangling off the hook,
the dial-tone expired.
People who don't listen to music
struggle at the vending machine,
their currency upside down,
their intended treat manacled
by the tight coil of the apparatus.
People who don't listen to music
suck imported, boutique plum pits.
People who don't listen to music
scoff at the buttered onion!

They attend registration drives
in circular parks
but withdraw after discovering that
they won't receive a gift,
such as a four-slice toaster
or a festive doilies four-pack.
They gnaw on the principles
of other generations
even as the principles
of other generations gnaw on them.
"Gnaw, man," says a jokester
from a jokester generation,
but the wordplay carouses briefly,
glancing off a plate-glass window.
They monitor their carotid arteries
during periods of inactivity,
often with concerning results,
such as mule-kick pulses
or blender-on-pulse, pulses.
People who don't listen to music
listen to people who don't listen to music.
They clasp their hands like "hurrahs,"
only they won't raise these "hurrahs"
over their heads, and their hands, unclasping,
approximate the weary countries
                              of sequestration.

What I Lost Was This:

"You said," you say, but I didn't say, and you reply, "You did," but I didn't do. Where does this leave us but in love? And what's love but a neighborhood of stoops (crumbling) and (artisanal) aimlessness.

A kid ran out of the park at 3:00 o'clock in the morning only to strike a taxicab. The kid bounced, without a shirt, the rent fabric of his breath in the freezing air. A passerby gave him socks. It wasn't unkind, exactly, but ill-fitting, emblematic of the post-industrial wasteland that saddens our generational critics.

There sat the kid, untying his shoes (still shirtless) beside the flashing hazard lights of the taxicab, tossing his own socks into the gutter, and replacing them with the warm, sweaty cottons from the donor. I had little to do but watch beneath a loud lamp. I'll never forget the band of agitated blue jays, four or five of them, stabbing the cold with the metallic tone of their vocabulary.

"Word, comma, your mama." Do you clarify? Yes, you clarify.

We were never happier (you and I) than when we were lying to each other. You texting me selfies on windy afternoons and me pretending to receive them an hour later. If I stood somewhere other than where I purported to stand, I did so out of fear, and in losing you, okay, what I lost was this:

[…] the bus stop is empty when the bus arrives. Instead, a worker sweeps old leaves into a dustpan. Why is the sinoatrial rhythm of our hearts keyed to the murmurs of thunder?

Why I Love Poets

I love poets because they'll phone me from a TJ Maxx dressing room—the muggy lighting, yes, the discarded sundresses, the sheer, sheer hosiery—only to imply that my leftist politics nevertheless don't equal their own tilted-beret Marxism. I love poets because they're always crashing at my apartment, stealing turns in the shower, and pooping out odd little evergreens into my toilet, but never acknowledging our friendship after they return to their academic jobs, or their NYC jobs, or their mysterious positions grooming information for dubious conglomerates. They are gymnasts, these poets; they leap onto dangerous ledges, their frigid synapses medicated against the pervasive societal forces that would otherwise embrace them gently or roughly as the case may be. They are beautiful and handsome alike; they copulate in ways that mimic the backstroke or sidestroke or how people ride a two-person (or three-person) bicycle.

I love poets, because they equate anti-Trump Facebook postings to "taking a stand" even as this passive behavior contributes to the "white noise" that obscures Trump's gateway fascism. Nobody is more qualified than poets when it comes to judging—arbitrating—the truth of a flawed system, and I love them, the poets, because we need them (finally, definitively) to scold us, to scald us with the righteousness we cannot perceive via our own faculties. They are poets, they compose poetry after all, it has rhyme and abstraction and non sequitur and metrical brilliance (at least what they dictate into a smartphone does), and after an appropriate interval, presses bind these poems into sheathes. Reluctantly, they read from these sheathes, they chant from these sheathes in doldrums known as 'iambics', but don't mistake their casual modesty at first, no, the poets aspire to give us readings, they are libraries unto themselves, they whip us with their oratory.

I love poets because they're the culprits behind a pattern of larcenies: the tip jar money, the vintage jacket, the autographed Tina Brooks album on Blue Note. They weep, the poets, while seated within the expanse of musty leather armchairs, the armchairs are endowed, they are named for other poets who wept in other armchairs, they wept, did the forebears, and they weep, do the contemporaries, for themselves, for their minimalist, pointillist dramaturgy, they weep until they are comforted by an administrator. There's nothing like a repentant poet, simply put, since there are no repentant poets, only the word repentance, the sound of which approaches, curiously enough, the sound of the word "serpents." I love poets, though, notwithstanding their record-setting selfishness, but because no other group of people can emerge from the cellars of isolation, after thirty minutes of exertion, wielding the high voltage of impregnable verse, and if I'm lucky, I should like to become just one such impossible person, a poet.

About the Author

Dan Gutstein is the author of *non/fiction* (stories, 2010), *Bloodcoal & Honey* (poems, 2011), and *Buildings Without Murders* (novel, 2020). His writing has appeared in more than 100 journals and anthologies, including *Ploughshares, American Scholar, Best American Poetry, The Penguin Book of the Sonnet, TriQuarterly, The Iowa Review,* and *Prairie Schooner.* He has been the recipient of grants and awards from the Bread Loaf Writers' Conference, the Maryland State Arts Council, UnitedStatesArtists, Women in Film & Video, and Emory University. In addition to writing activities, he is vocalist for punk band Joy on Fire, who will be performing a Tiny Desk Concert at NPR, and co-director of a forthcoming documentary film, *Li'l Liza Jane: The Story of America Through the History of a Song.* At present, he is a nomad, dividing his time between the crashable couches of Trenton, N.J. and other scenic overlooks.

About the Press

Unsolicited Press was founded in 2012 and is based in Portland, Oregon. The press produces stellar fiction, nonfiction, and poetry from award-winning writers. Authors include John W. Bateman, T.K. Lee, Rosalia Scalia, and Brook Bhagat.

Find the press on Twitter and Instagram: @unsolicitedp

Learn more at www.unsolicitedpress.com.

www.ingramcontent.com/pod-product-compliance
Lightning Source LLC
LaVergne TN
LVHW040108080526
838202LV00045B/3820